fatherhood

fatherhood

CHARLES PHILLIPS

illustrations by Mandy Pritty

RYLAND
PETERS
& SMALL
LONDON NEW YORK

For Melanie, Jim, and Tom

Design Pamela Daniels and Fiona Tweedie
Editor Miriam Hyslop
Production Patricia Harrington
Art Director Gabriella Le Grazie
Publishing Director Alison Starling

Editorial Consultant Christina Rodenbeck

First published in
the United States in 2004 by
Ryland Peters & Small, Inc.
519 Broadway
5th Floor
New York NY 10012
www.rylandpeters.com

10 9 8 7 6 5 4 3 2 1

Text, design, and commissioned
photographs © Ryland Peters & Small 2004

Jacket credits: Back jacket below
photography by Debi Treloar

Printed in China

ISBN 1 84172 596 X

Cataloging-in-Publication Data
is available from the Library of
Congress on request.

contents

introduction

*Life's aspirations come
in the form of children.*

RABINDRANATH TAGORE (1861–1941)

The joys of parents are secret, and so are
their griefs and fears: they cannot utter the one,
nor they will not utter the other.

FRANCIS BACON (1561–1626)

The day you become a father will live with you forever. Your baby son or daughter transforms your view of the world, delivering you to an unfamiliar place and demanding that you learn a difficult but richly fulfilling role. Perhaps as you hold your newborn baby, you will consider the movement of generations in a family—and view your father with fresh eyes as you contemplate occupying the position he took for you. For many of us, fatherhood brings us closer to our fathers—it helps us to see them, if we have not before, as people like us facing up to challenging circumstances as best they can.

The day your son or daughter is born begins a thrilling years-long dance of discovery for you both. Across decades you are bound by an intense father/child bond, a love that survives many vicissitudes. They say that in these times of fast-changing working practices being a father is the last "job for life." When you become a father, there is no going back. You cannot flee, but there is a fierce joy in that. You may not feel ready for the responsibility, but your heart is bursting with love.

Our birth is but a sleep and a forgetting:
The Soul that rises with us, our life's Star,
Hath had elsewhere its setting,
And cometh from afar;
Not in entire forgetfulness,
And not in utter nakedness,
But trailing clouds of glory do we come
From God, who is our home:
Heaven lies about us in our infancy!
Shades of the prison-house begin to close
Upon the growing boy
But he beholds the light, and whence it flows,
He sees it in his joy;
The youth, who daily farther from the east
Must travel, still is Nature's priest,
And by the vision splendid
Is on his way attended;
At length the man perceives it die away,
And fade into the light of common day.

WILLIAM WORDSWORTH (1770–1850)

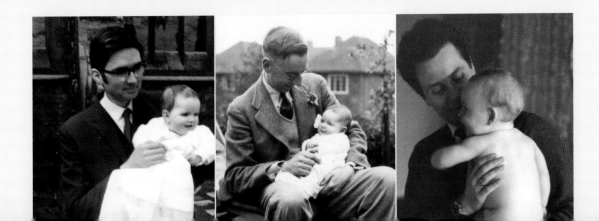

anticipation

If I were alone in the desert and feeling afraid,
I would want a child alongside me.
For then my fear would fade away
And I would be made strong.

MEISTER ECKHART (c.1260 – c.1327)

...And all to leave what with his toil he won
To that unfeather'd two-legged thing, a son.

JOHN DRYDEN (1631–1700)

 sperm power

There is an average of 280 million sperm in each ejaculation.

fertility icons

In Britain the Celts believed that the horned god Cernunnos and the hammer-bearer Sucellus held power over fertility. The Celts also carved evocative temple images of cloaked deities (called *genii cucullati*—"hooded figures") often shown carrying eggs, underlining their links to bodily fertility.

Among the ancient Aztecs, prospective parents prayed to Tezcatlipoca, who protected pregnant women, and Tlazolteotl, goddess of childbirth. Carved images of Tlazolteotl depict her in the act of giving birth.

choosing to **become a father**

The news that you are becoming a father may be a joyful surprise, a long-awaited breakthrough, or a shock. Perhaps you have been planning for this happy event, buying equipment, decorating a nursery at home. You may have just begun trying to start a family—or have given no thought at all to the matter.

Even if you've been longing for this news, you're bound to feel a little trepidation. Perhaps you are unsure that you're ready to care for a child or be a role model for this developing individual. But equally you probably feel a sweep of nervous excitement. If all goes well, in a few short months you will hold in your hands a new generation of your family—a tiny bundle that will fill you with awe at the preciousness and fragility of life.

the next step

You have reached a point in your life at which becoming a father seems the right next step. Perhaps you have recently married, or you and your partner have come to the realization that you would like to share your life with children. The adventure of becoming parents is a wonderful experience to share with your partner or wife, a joyful flowering of your relationship. It gives you a chance to grow together as individuals and as a couple.

For many women the desire to be a mother is intimately bound up with their female identity. Men usually experience the drive to have offspring less strongly—at least in their youth. But they often find that becoming a father and caring for the baby is a powerfully moving experience that resonates at a deep level within them.

Becoming a parent makes you feel fiercely alive. At the same time, witnessing the pain of your partner's labor, and holding your baby's tiny body, you are aware of the closeness of death even at the beginnings of life.

Accidents will happen in the best regulated families.

CHARLES DICKENS (1812–1870)

accidents will happen

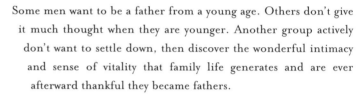

Some men want to be a father from a young age. Others don't give it much thought when they are younger. Another group actively don't want to settle down, then discover the wonderful intimacy and sense of vitality that family life generates and are ever afterward thankful they became fathers.

The news that your partner is pregnant may have taken you by surprise. The prospect of beginning family life in eight or nine months' time is unsettling: you will have to change your plans. But often life's richest experiences come unexpectedly.

Give yourself time to adjust your perspective, and try to be honest with yourself. Try to connect to your deepest sense of who you are and what you want. If you looked down on yourself from a position outside time or at the end of your life, what would your priorities be? If you shift your perspective from immediate concerns about money or your career, you may find that what you want is no longer at odds with the prospect of becoming a father.

Deep in the cave of the baby's breast
Hides the father's nature, ready for new life.

HORACE (65–8BC)

 british fathers are getting older

The average age of a father when his child is registered has risen from just over 27 in 1971 to just over 30 in 1999.

 strong swimmer

It takes a sperm 6 hours to reach the woman's egg.

listening to the biological clock

Men can become fathers at an advanced age—even in our 80s and 90s, we can father children. The "biological clock" forces women in their 30s to take a "soon or never" approach to motherhood, but it ticks much more quietly for men at this age. But bear in mind that age makes a difference for men, too. Caring for babies and juggling work and family life can be very demanding. You will find it easier to cope at 33 than you will at 43—and easier at 43 than at 53 or 63.

fear vs. excitement

cheers

52 baby girls in England and Wales were named "Chardonnay" in 2002—perhaps a tribute to a character in a popular and glamorous TV drama *Footballers' Wives*. Another 14 babies were named "Chardonay."

aztec names

In Aztec families, a boy would be named after his grandfather or father—usually an active name such as Chimalpopoca (Smoking Crest). Girls were given more evocative, poetic names taken from the natural world—for example, Quiau-xochitl (Rainflower).

Think of your father. Was he distant, always too busy to talk to you or play with you? Was he always traveling for his job, so that you felt you hardly saw him? Perhaps you were lucky and he grasped the opportunity of being a parent with both hands, offering you warm, spontaneous attention and unconditional love. Your own childhood is likely to loom large as you look forward to the baby's arrival.

Some fathers see being a parent as an opportunity to right the wrongs of their own childhood. If you were disappointed by how you were treated, this is your chance to do things differently. If you think your father was too strict and authoritarian, you can take a more lenient and cooperative approach with your own child.

You re-enter the world of childhood with your own children—you will be inspired by the joy your toddler takes in looking, by the intensity of your baby daughter's attention as she watches the sunlight falling on the kitchen wall. Your baby will re-magic the world, restoring you to a state of intense interest, the level of captivated attention you have when you see something really new—on the first day of a vacation in a surprising and wonderful place. You can share with her in the beauty of small things.

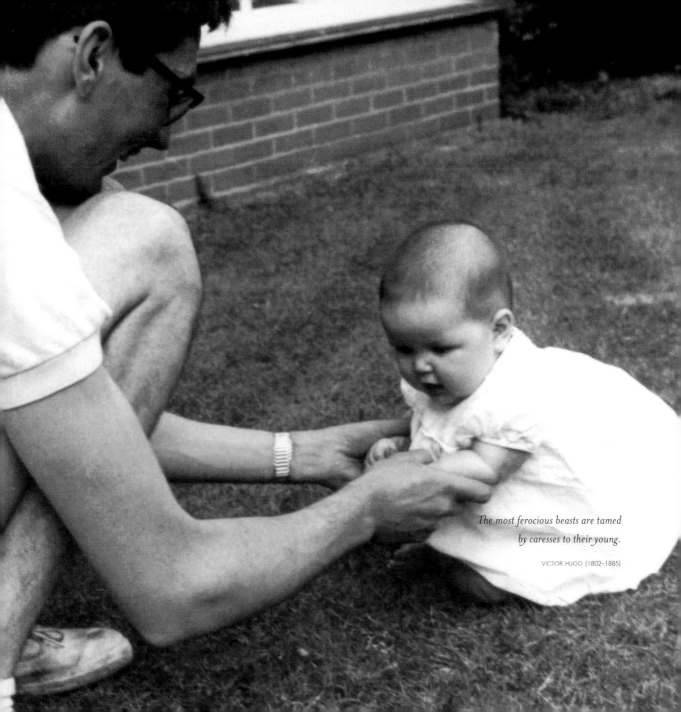

The most ferocious beasts are tamed by caresses to their young.

VICTOR HUGO (1802–1885)

The truly great man never turns
away a child's simplicity.

CONFUCIUS (551–479BC)

sudden responsibility

At first the idea of being a father may seem daunting. Fear can be the dominant emotion—that you will somehow fail the baby, that you will never manage to provide for her, that you will repeat a bad pattern from your own upbringing. How will you manage to balance the demands of work and family life? How will you know what to do as a parent?

But one of the joys of fatherhood is that it forces you to take responsibility. It's up to you. Try to have confidence in yourself. Think back to other events that once seemed impossibly daunting—making a major presentation, starting a new job, or going to a new school. You were probably surprised by the resources you discovered then. When you hold your own son in your hands, when you take as full a part as you can in his life—bathing, carrying, perhaps bottle-feeding—you will make an intense connection with him that will draw out the inner strength that you possess.

 your children need you

90 percent of Americans believe that fathers make "a unique contribution" to the lives of their children.

 final fling

Just as newlyweds mark the passage from single to married life with bachelorette parties and stag nights, so it is a good idea to arrange a final fling of your life before fatherhood and mother-hood. After the baby is born, it may be some time before you and your partner have an extended period alone together. Before she becomes very heavily pregnant, make time for a vacation together. If possible, go somewhere you have always wanted to visit together. Or indulge yourselves in burst of favorite activities that it will be difficult to enjoy together when the baby is with you. For example, arrange a weekend hiking, scuba diving, or visit art galleries and exhibitions.

"Wait till your father gets home"

You are probably luckier than your father and certainly luckier than your grandfather. Men and women in recent generations were generally bound by fairly rigid ideas of the behavior that was appropriate to the different sexes. At one time men were expected to be breadwinners for their stay-at-home wives, and when they came home, they were likely to disappear with a stiff drink behind a newspaper and emerge only to discipline naughty sons and daughters. Fatherhood was seen less in terms of its joy than of its responsibilities—to provide a decent standard of living and a firm hand of authority for your offspring.

Your life as a father is much more likely to involve extended periods of looking after your child. You will have the chance to get to know your baby and, later, child. You may share the responsibility for earning a living with your wife or partner. If you are sensible, you and your partner will divide the job of applying discipline. You will get the full experience of being a parent—the intense joy of connecting with your baby will lighten the feeling of responsibility.

Children deserve the greatest respect. If you are considering a shameful act, do not ignore your child's youthful years.

JUVENAL (C.55–C.140)

the big cigar

A baby is an angel whose wings shrink as his legs grow.

FRENCH PROVERB

 wetting the baby's head

In western cultures the first ritual celebration of a birth is often the wetting of the baby's head —marking the new arrival by drinking a toast to his health.

what can he see?

A newborn baby can focus and follow a moving object such as your finger with his eyes. But he can't focus on objects more than 10–15 inches away.

He'll copy movements of your lips and tongue.

He can hear—he looks as if he's listening when someone speaks to him. Babies are particularly programmed to respond to female voices because a woman offers the promise of milk.

He can distinguish and be comforted by familiar smells—such as the smell of his mother or father.

And as you discover almost at once, he can communicate loudly and insistently—by crying.

falling in love

The long wait of the pregnancy and the difficult hours of labor are over. Your partner has been given her newborn son to hold. Together you share in his very first moments in the world.

As you pick him up for the first time, it is a deeply charged and elemental moment. You may feel a sense of great pride and awe to be holding your child. If you were lucky enough to have been with your partner through her labor, you're probably feeling emotionally drained after witnessing her pain. Your baby looks tiny and vulnerable. A new life has begun. It does seem as if a miracle has occurred.

Some fathers experience a strong connection with the baby, others feel more detached from the event. Here, and throughout the years of parenting, don't beat yourself up for not being a perfect parent. Give it your best shot. Over the first weeks of baby's life strengthen your connection to the baby by spending as much time with him as you can.

It is true that a child is always hungry all over; but he is also curious all over, and his curiosity is excited about as early as his hunger.

CHARLES DUDLEY WARNER (1829–1900)

breastfeeding

Breastfeeding is difficult for some mothers, but your support can be vital. American research shows that women who are actively supported by their partners in breastfeeding continue breast-feeding their babies for longer than those who are not supported.

circumcision

In some African tribes, boys are circumcised as a rite of passage from boyhood into adulthood. Jewish boys are circumcised at the age of eight days. The practice is in honor of God's covenant with Abraham in which he promised lands to Abraham's descendants. Muslim boys are circumcised as a sign of devotion to Allah.

work to live?

Three-quarters of British men aged under 55 say they place a higher priority than their fathers did on achieving a balance between work and home life.

Infancy conforms to nobody;
all conform to it.

RALPH WALDO EMERSON (1803–1882)

a little **competitor**

Your partner will be intensely involved with the baby over the first few weeks, and you may feel excluded as you watch mother and baby bond. For some men the baby begins to seem like a rival—your partner no longer has time or interest in anything but the baby, and it can be difficult to make a speedy adjustment after the intense intimacy of late pregnancy and the birth itself. Here it is important to be as involved as you can in caring for the baby—the more you do, the closer you will feel to him.

If you can, take a couple of weeks off work at the start of the baby's life. He may be restless at night and disrupt your sleeping patterns. It greatly reduces tension at this time if you—and your partner—are not worrying about having to be up early to jump in the car or catch the train.

If you and your partner are bottle-feeding rather than breastfeeding the baby, you have a great opportunity—try to feed him or her whenever possible. You will find your connection with the baby immeasurably strengthened if you regularly feed him or her.

Volunteer as often as you can to spend time with the baby, bathe him, change his diaper, and ease him into sleep. Researchers investigating what makes a healthy family have found that when a father takes a hands-on role in nurturing his baby, it has a positive effect on the child's sense of security and wellbeing later in life.

There was never a child so lovely but his mother was glad to get him asleep.

RALPH WALDO EMERSON (1803–1882)

*You have a lifetime of work,
but your children are only young once.*

POLISH PROVERB

dada! the first year

Time flies by. The days—at least the hours you spend at home—are filled with new experiences. Before you know it, your daughter is a year old. Every minute of waking time she has been experimenting with her surroundings and learning from the world. In the first year of her life, she develops from a heartrendingly defenseless bundle to a strong-legged toddler who has already mastered the beginnings of speech. You'll already have a clear sense of her personality.

daddy play

Fathers are not substitute mothers. Research has shown that being nurtured by father as well as by mother makes a baby feel particularly safe, loved, and cared for. You and your partner respond to your baby in distinctive ways—your baby needs you both. Fathers tend to play more boisterous, physical games with babies, toddlers, and children. This is good for your son and daughter, it gives them confidence and a safe arena for testing their strength and coordination. Do bear in mind the effect of disrupting a quiet bedtime ritual. If you arrive home from work and engage your daughter in boisterous games, you can't expect her to go to sleep ten minutes later when you are ready for a glass of wine and your dinner. Save the dangling and rolling games for morning.

 changing tastes

A 1972 US study plotted how babies enjoy different "baby games" more at certain ages. Peek-a-boo got no laughs at 4 months, but made 55 percent of babies laugh at 7 months. Kissing the baby's tummy was always popular, but the biggest hit at 7 months (77 percent laughed). Hide and seek—hiding one of your baby's toys, then revealing it—was most popular at 10 months.

We find delight in the beauty and happiness of children that makes the heart too big for the body.

RALPH WALDO EMERSON (1803–1882)

 inca naming

Among the Incas, naming did not take place until puberty. For the first two years of life, a child was called simply wawa (baby), then was given a temporary name until he or she took a permanent name at around 14.

the christening

If you belong to a broadly Christian family, you may choose to have your baby christened. Christening ceremonies provide a focus for a family party to celebrate the baby's birth and introduce him to more distant family members. In a christening service, the baby is welcomed into some Christian churches through the rite of baptism—a minister blesses water and pours a little over the baby's head. The baby is also publicly given her name. Two friends or relatives of the parents take vows to be "godparents" who will make sure the baby has an ethical and religious upbringing.

the wider **family**

As you get to grips with being a father, your extended family can be either a help or a hindrance. Depending on how well you get along with your own father and mother and your partner's close relatives, you may welcome or be irritated by their presence and advice.

Perhaps you have clear ideas about the way your father and mother behaved toward you and the kind of parent you want to be, or you feel overwhelmed by your new status as a father and thrown into self-doubt. We can probably all learn from the experience of older parents, but it's important for our self-esteem and for parenting consistency for us to decide on and follow our own path as fathers.

The members of the extended family will probably play an important part in your child's later years. As you know from your own childhood, grandparents, uncles, and aunts are often treasured friends to a child, offering a listening ear and a different perspective on family or school problems. Most fathers will welcome offers of practical help from family and in-laws, unless the relationship is very strained.

The Boys take all after their Father,
and covet to tread in his steps;
yea, if they do but see any place where
the old Pilgrim hath lain, or any print of
his foot, it ministreth joy to their hearts,
and they covet to lie or tread in the same.

JOHN BUNYAN (1628–1688)

two-home parenting

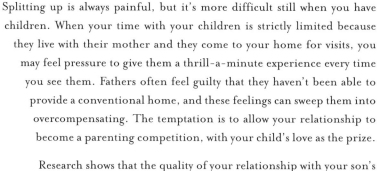

Splitting up is always painful, but it's more difficult still when you have children. When your time with your children is strictly limited because they live with their mother and they come to your home for visits, you may feel pressure to give them a thrill-a-minute experience every time you see them. Fathers often feel guilty that they haven't been able to provide a conventional home, and these feelings can sweep them into overcompensating. The temptation is to allow your relationship to become a parenting competition, with your child's love as the prize.

Research shows that the quality of your relationship with your son's mother is among the most important contributors to his healthy development. The better you two adults can get along, the better your son will fare. Making peace with your ex may be painful, but it will be a labor of love for your son—and in the long run should help your own wellbeing. Conflict with your ex-partner puts pressure on you and on your son, but the more relaxed you and he can be, the more you will both enjoy yourselves.

If you cannot be near your children, they will still benefit from having access to you. Even if you're in a different city, with a demanding job, your relationship with your distant children can thrive, provided you make time to call them, write to them, email them—and be available for them to reply. Arrange a regular time at which they can call you or get a pager so you can break off what you're doing, if possible, to take their call.

two families under one roof

Fathers who live with children and stepchildren also face demanding pressures. Their temptation may be to treat their own children differently from their stepchildren—either by indulging them as favorites or by being extra strict with them. There are often added tensions that arise because their children don't or won't get along with their stepmothers, or with their stepbrothers and -sisters. Being open and honest should bring benefits—admit to your own feelings and difficulties, and be as accessible as you can.

 one-parent wonders

68 percent of US children lived with two parents in 1999, a drop from the 1980 figure of 77 percent.

23 percent lived only with mothers, 4 percent only with their fathers, 4 percent with neither parent.

 back to school

1997 research carried out in Washington, DC, showed that when fathers were involved in children's schooling, the children did much better at school—they enjoyed class more, got better grades, and were less likely to be suspended or expelled. The children also seemed to have better standing in class.

 separation stats

In the US six out of ten divorcing couples have children, and 1 million American children experience their parents' divorce each year.

fathers & sons

His little son into his bosom creeps
The lively picture of his father's face.

PHINEAS FLETCHER (1582–1650)

Story time is a chance to strengthen your bond with your son. Reading to him will also develop his imagination and his language and recognition skills. You can start with tough water-proof books he can try to eat or sit on in the bath. Try books with textured panels or bright patterns, or ones with photographs of babies crawling, standing, and eating. Your son will soon let you know his favorite—and he'll want to read it again and again. As he gets older, you can move on to musical books, books with push-button speech, and pull-a-tab books with elaborate moving parts.

It is a wise father that knows his own child.

WILLIAM SHAKESPEARE (1564–1616)

a chip off the old block

When you hold your son in your hands, you see your own immortality. For a moment you can dream of defying death, because you are holding a part of yourself that, barring tragedy, will live on after you die. When your son was born, you were transformed from your father's son to your son's father. Now you wonder whether he will become a father himself, transforming you once more, from father to grandfather.

You see yourself in your son. You may be troubled by echoes of your own personality or immeasurably proud that he takes after you in some way. But you need to be careful not to impose your own qualities on him. As children grow older, fathers—and mothers—are sometimes drawn into projecting their anxieties or even their own bad qualities onto their children. We should try to accept our children for what they are. It is fun to share our enthusiasms with our sons, and to dream about their future achievements, but we will benefit from making a conscious effort to see past ourselves and view them in a clear light. Let your son develop his own unique personality, and take pride in himself, for only in this way will he find the fulfillment you want for him.

As fathers we should try to avoid a "do what I say, not what I do" approach. We are role models for our sons—our behavior provides the pattern they use to build their sense of self. We can teach them far more effectively and memorably by doing than by telling. By seeing you behave with consideration for other people, for example, your son will learn to think of others' feelings.

I do not love him because he behaves well,
but simply because he is my little son.

RABINDRANATH TAGORE (1861–1941)

out in the world

From the moment your son is born and the umbilical cord is cut, you and his mother begin the process of socializing him—helping him fit into the wider world. As father, one of your most important tasks is to make him feel secure enough to cope with being separated from her—and you.

The more you can be involved in looking after him the better—you can give him a positive first experience of being separated from his mother. And the more you can boost his sense that he is loved and accepted at all times, the more self-reliant and secure he is likely to be.

 caring children

A 26-year study found that children whose fathers had been closely involved in their upbringing showed more concern than other children for the feelings of others.

 first day at school

His first day at school will bring mixed emotions. You will feel trepidation—imagine how big and forbidding the school seems to him. How will he cope with the long day, the rules, the sea of unfamiliar faces? You may feel excited, too, and proud to see him marching in, facing up to this challenge. You may want him to be braver than he is, and feel embarrassed by his clinging to your legs, hiding his face in your jacket.

※ multiple dads

Some aboriginal peoples in Africa, Australasia, and South America believe that a baby can have more than one biological father—they think that two or more sexual acts can contribute to the creation of an embryo. In some groups, when a baby is born to a woman who has had sex with more than one man around the time when she conceived, she names the men she slept with as joint fathers. If they accept that they are fathers, they share the responsibility for supporting and caring for the child. Research published in 2002 showed that children with more than one father in these societies tend to thrive—among the Bari people of Venezuela, 80 percent of children with two or more fathers survive to adulthood compared to 64 percent of single-father children.

Only happy people can make a happy world.

BUDDHIST SAYING

days out

A key aspect of your role as father is to be a playmate—to teach by doing, and sharing activities. Regular days out are a good opportunity to connect with your son in this practical way. These outings can be focused on his interests, but they also give you a chance to introduce him to your hobbies. As he gets a little older, he'll probably love sharing your passion for fly-fishing, basketball, or hiking.

Days out are also a time for you to encourage him to take and enjoy exercise. Many inner-city schools have to make do without playgrounds and children may not get much chance to have regular exercise outside of ordinary school playtime. Good exercise habits will safeguard his young heart and stand him in good stead for later life. Your encouragement could be a vital help to establishing these habits.

From early in his life, it's good to plan outings with other fathers. Sharing time with other fathers, can help you gain a fresh perspective on your relationship with your son by watching how he interacts with other boys and other men. You may be able to help with any problems you can see. Sometimes as your son gets older, it can be good for both you and him to take a step back from your own one-to-one relationship in this wider friendship.

becoming a young man

shooting up

Adolescent boys usually have a growth spurt between 10 and 13.

During his growth spurt your son may grow 4 inches in height in a year.

"i'm sleeping"

Adolescent boys need more sleep than children or adults.

crashes and bumps

Hormonal changes tend to make adolescent boys physically clumsy.

The intense, involving love you feel for your growing son is complicated by the ways he reminds you of yourself, which can provoke a mixture of pride and displeasure, often working at deep and barely recognized levels. These emotions become more complicated still as he nears manhood. The temptation to interfere, to stop him from making your mistakes, may have been present all along but will inevitably grow stronger as he gets older. Your son wants to feel that he is loved by you for who he is rather than your idea of who or what he should be.

Research shows that family authority works best if children feel they are consulted as much as possible. Simply imposing orders from on high may work in the army, but it breeds resistance and resentment in the family context. Your son is more likely to accept your authority if he feels you are willing to negotiate with him. He will resist you—this is part of defining himself, and you probably wouldn't want it any other way. But he also needs to know that there is a point beyond which he cannot go.

teen spirit

Adolescence is a difficult time. We can probably remember the horrors of our own adolescence—but not from our parents' perspective! Our sons may become—it seems to us—surly, combative, clumsy, slobbish, lazy. We have to respond. As at many times throughout the journey of parenthood, we should be wary of transferring our own half-understood failings to them. We will benefit from taking a step back—if you feel you have tendencies to be lazy, when you see your son being lazy it will "push your buttons." In the minefield of adolescence experts recommend having a few agreed rules and keeping strictly to them. Don't make a stand over unimportant things and then have to back down. With regard to sex, drugs, and alcohol, you may lose your son's trust if you overstate your case. Be clear and honest about your feelings regarding these issues.

Fathers should not get too deeply discouraged when their son rejects their advice ... years later the son will pass it on to his own offspring.

ANON

a strong drink

Among the Kikuyu tribe of Africa, boys are initiated into manhood by drinking the blood of the male tribesmen. They are taken away from their mothers and the village to an isolated spot, where they are kept for three days of fasting and preparation. Then they join the male group around a fire. All the men cut their forearm and allow some of their lifeblood to flow into a bowl they are passing around. Men and boys all drink from the bowl to signify that they are united and committed to one another.

bar mitzvah

Some religious groups still have ritual rites of passage. In the Jewish religion, a boy has his Bar Mitzvah at age 13 to mark his arrival as an adult male worshipper. Usually on the Sabbath following his 13th birthday, he is called out during the religious service to read from the Torah (the first five books of the Hebrew Bible), and he sometimes then gives an address to the assembled worshippers. After the service there is usually a Kiddush ceremony (a prayer over a cup of wine) followed by a family celebration. After his Bar Mitzvah the boy is counted as an adult for religious worship and has the right to wear phylacteries (religious symbols) on the forehead and left arm.

daddy's girl

I have done nothing
but in care of thee—
Of thee, my dear one!
Thee, my daughter!

WILLIAM SHAKESPEARE (1564–1616)

getting wrapped **around her finger**

As you hold your baby daughter in your hands, you are profoundly aware of her newness and fragility. Yet her tiny body has the capacity to give life. Will she one day go through the labor you have just witnessed and become a mother?

Many fathers find their connection with their daughters has a different quality to their relationship with their sons. In your son you may see more of yourself than you do in your daughter. You are involved with his struggles and his developing personality in a direct way because they connect to memories of your own childhood. You may want him to be different with intense energy because of your sense of your own failings. Your love for your daughter has a different perspective. You'll probably find yourself being more indulgent of a daughter than of a son. You may feel a protective gallantry, a desire to pile your love high for her, to pave her path with good things.

your daughter and her mother

You daughter is a mystery. You cannot know her as you know your son. One of the driving elements of your adult relationship with her mother is the difference between you, and the energy of this male/female distinction also colors your relationship with your daughter. Perhaps you feel you don't understand her. Particularly as your daughter grows older, you may find there are more secret areas of her life than there are with a son.

She may develop a particular affinity with her mother, seemingly wanting to spend time with her more than she does with you. You may feel rejected, but underneath the daughter/father bond remains strong as ever.

To progress in life she needs to feel deeply loved and supported by you both, and you have a particular role in boosting her self-esteem and social confidence. Make sure she knows she is beautiful in your eyes and loved by you no matter what may happen.

A little girl with no doll is nearly
as unlucky and quite as impossible
as a woman with no children.

VICTOR HUGO (1802–1885)

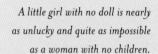

beautiful locks

Among the Incas, a girl's passage into womanhood at puberty was marked with a public hair combing ceremony.

first communion

For Roman Catholic children the first Communion service is an important rite of passage, marking the child's welcome into the adult church. Children attend catechism classes in which they learn the doctrine of the church for several weeks before the ceremony. They normally take their first Communion between the ages of eight and 12. Girls usually dress in white, often with a veil, while boys also wear elaborate outfits. Boys and girls take great pleasure in being the center of attraction, but for some girls it is particularly exciting since it allows them to dress up almost as if for a wedding. During the ceremony the children have their first experience of Holy Communion, in which Catholics believe the bread eaten in the ceremony becomes the body of Jesus Christ. It can be a powerfully moving moment for all involved.

He who has daughters is always a shepherd.

 sex roles

US research shows that most girls who had premarital sex said that their mother and father had strictly traditional views of male and female roles.

 a third of the job

2003 statistics reveal that British fathers now carry out one-third of childcare.

tomboy charm

As your daughter gets older, she may seem to need you less than she did when you had to be on guard all the time in case she fell or put something dangerous in her mouth. But your familiar, reliable love is a great comfort as she embarks on her first friendships, her first months and years at school, her first trip away from home—to her aunt's or grandmother's, say. Now it is necessary to take a few steps away from her, to be willing to fade a little into the background. You are like an old jacket for her. She may take you off, but she needs you as much as ever when it gets cold.

the tomboy

Does she come in with rips in her clothes and mud on her knees? Does she love to climb trees? If she enjoys a "tomboy phase," your daughter may go from playing with dolls to scrapping with groups of boys.

Many fathers and mothers are amazed to find that girls and boys seem to be preprogrammed in their play. You make a special effort not to impose any boy/girl stereotypes on their behavior, yet you find the girls playing with dolls and the boys careering around pretending twigs are guns. When your daughter plays like a tomboy, is she experimenting with stereotypes, or is she just playing in whatever way feels right? Probably a bit of both.

This is a time when fathers and daughters can grow close. If she's trying out being a tomboy, she's likely to want to share in your interests—invite her along when you go fishing or hiking, to a football or basketball game.

There is evidence that children thrive in families where mothers and fathers share the traditional male/female roles. It appears to help children feel secure enough to plot their own path if they are able to see their parents as an alliance of equals, who share caring and nurturing as well as responsibility.

Trust not your daughters' minds
By what you see them act.

WILLIAM SHAKESPEARE (1564–1616)

images of women

*Precious to a young girl's heart
is her own charm and beauty.*

OVID (43BC–AD17)

In Western society we concentrate fanatically on women's appearance. Movie actresses have to follow rigid diets and resort to cosmetic surgery to stay in shape for the top parts. In newspapers and magazines, high-flying business and academic women are paraded and judged on their looks. Compared to looking good, everything else comes second. The effects of this celebrity culture on girls can be extremely distressing. Research shows that rising numbers are dieting even before the age of 10, and one in a hundred 12 to 18 year-olds fall prey to the eating disorder anorexia nervosa. Parents cannot take on the culture singlehanded.

But as a father you have a special role to play in making your daughter feel secure and loveable. You begin when she is an infant—your hugs express the warmth of your protective love. As she gets older you can try by always giving her your full, undivided attention to make her feel valued for who she is. Over time her sense of being complete and loveable will build up, and should help her when she has to face insecurities over how people will see her, how they will judge her appearance.

By the time she is 10 or 11, she may be quite conscious of fashions. You'll probably find yourself complimenting her on her appearance. You'll want her to feel good about the way she looks. But you may want to strike a balance between boosting her confidence and reinforcing any developing obsessions about looking good.

Sir, I love you more than word can wield the matter;

Dearer than eye-sight, space and liberty;

Beyond what can be valued, rich or rare;

No less than life, with grace, health, beauty, honour;

As much as child e'er lov'd, or father found;

A love that makes breath poor and speech unable;

Beyond all manner of so much I love you.

WILLIAM SHAKESPEARE (1564–1616)

the boyfriend

As your daughter grows older, your protective instincts may grow stronger than ever. As she hits the years 10–12, then becomes a teenager, goes through puberty, has to deal with social pressures at school, wants to go out at night with her friends, perhaps finds a boyfriend, your mind will be racing through all the things that could go wrong. Your impulse may be to hold her back and keep her safe. But equally you know she has to be allowed to find her feet, to make her own mistakes. If she has to learn any lessons, they will be lessons of experience rather than ones you have handed down.

This does not mean that you—and her mother—should not take precautions. Explain what could go wrong. Teach her how to protect herself. If you think she will encounter sex, alcohol, even drugs, be open, clear, and honest about potential danger. If you try to scare her into being "good" it may backfire. She is at an age when she must experiment. Equally your daughter needs—and wants—you to set limits. She doesn't want too much freedom all at once. If you are too easygoing, she may decide you don't really care about her. She is likely to interpret your lax attitude as a lack of love.

If you are raising your daughter on your own—or if you live apart from her mother and don't know what approach she is taking with you daughter—you'll probably want help from a sister or female friend. You may feel uncomfortable discussing the changes of puberty. Perhaps you feel you don't know how to advise her to take sensible precautions. Your daughter should have advice and support from women at this time.

 the first date

Your daughter's first date may make you may feel proud, apprehensive, and probably a little sad. This is one of the moments in her life that brings home to you how quickly time has passed since you held her as a tiny baby in your hands. There is no going back to her infancy— you once filled her world, but now she is replacing you; the forward movement of time makes you less important, brings you closer to death. You may not like her boyfriend. He'll probably see you as an enemy. But you know, equally, that it is right for her to move on. Try to take pleasure in the fact that you have done a good job in bringing her to the threshold of her adult life.

grown-ups

We cannot always build the future for our youth,
but we can build our youth for the future.

FRANKLIN D. ROOSEVELT (1882–1945)

*There is not so much comfort in the having of children
as there is sorrow in parting with them.*

THOMAS FULLER (1654–1734)

letting go

The day comes when your sons and daughters move on into adulthood.
This is a challenging time for any father, for you have to reinvent
your relationship with them. They are no longer children, and you
have to find it in yourself to relinquish them to life.

This transition will be easier for both of you if you have had an
easy and cooperative relationship with your children. If, as they
grow up, you consult them, negotiate with them, and trust them,
you will give them confidence in their ability to make their own
way. And it will be easier for you to let them go into adulthood
because you will have seen that they can cope with responsibility
and can stand on their own feet.

But even though you know they are no longer children, you will
always be their father, and they still need you to be available to
help. It is satisfying to be able to help them financially or
practically—with housing or a job—or to take them on vacation if
they are short of money.

Of course they may not want or need your help. Then it is
important to make sure that they can call on you if and when they
need you. Whatever happens in these years, there is an
unbreakable link between you that is no less strong now than it was
when you held your baby son or your daughter and they were small
enough to fit in your two hands. You are not in the foreground,
or the middle distance, but the background—on call, if needed.

 boys stay home

In 1999–2000 53 percent of British
men aged 20–24 were living with
their parents. Thirty-seven percent
of British women in this age group
were living in their parents' homes.

 festive reunions

As fathers we have an important
role to play in family get-togethers
on special occasions. If we try to
focus on the children, listening
to them with our full attention, and
treating them as adults, it will go a
long way toward making the
event a success.

... *my blessing with thee!*

And these few precepts in thy memory

Look thou character. Give thy thoughts no tongue,

Nor any unproportioned thought his act.

Be thou familiar, but by no means vulgar.

Those friends thou hast, and their adoption tried,

Grapple them to thy soul with hoops of steel;

But do not dull thy palm with entertainment

Of each new-hatch'd, unfledged comrade. Beware

Of entrance to a quarrel, but being in,

Bear't that the opposed may beware of thee

Give every man thy ear, but few thy voice;

Take each man's censure, but reserve thy judgment.

Costly thy habit as thy purse can buy,

But not express'd in fancy; rich, not gaudy;

For the apparel oft proclaims the man,

And they in France of the best rank and station

Are most select and generous, chief in that.

Neither a borrower, nor a lender be;

For loan oft loses both itself and friend,

And borrowing dulls the edge of husbandry.

This above all: to thine own self be true,

And it must follow, as the night the day,

Thou canst not then be false to any man.

Farewell: my blessing season this in thee!

WILLIAM SHAKESPEARE (1564–1616)

need for **mutual respect**

If your son's adolescence has gone well, you've probably had several head-on clashes with him. Your daughter may have pushed you to the edge of your patience. They have had to work against you and their mother to establish themselves; they needed you to be a fixed point that they could push against in defining their own position. You were changing, too, at this time, but they probably didn't notice—they may not have paid much attention to anything but themselves for a few years.

But now adolescence is past. They are moving into adulthood, and are probably ready to make friends with you. A major part of a father's love lies in letting go of all those teenage clashes, and being ready to be a different kind of parent in these years of adulthood. As they make their way in the world, they will make mistakes. You may be tempted to intervene—either to prevent things from going wrong or to tell them in strong language how they have messed up and must do better next time. But they have to make their mistakes—remember that the most valuable lessons you learned were born of experience.

If your daughter chooses to marry, you may experience the joy of being present at her wedding—perhaps of walking her down the aisle to "give her away" to the bridegroom in the marriage ceremony. In this resonant moment a father's heart swells with the satisfaction of having completed the demanding but immensely fulfilling journey from his daughter's babyhood to her departure now into adult life.

the next generation

In time you give way to your children. By a gradual process they take the center stage while you remain in support. You may retire or scale down your working life. Probably your son or daughter is very busy with work and can only visit you from time to time. Your thoughts will remain full of your children, but you will realize that the large part of your work as a father is done. You may feel a sense of loss, a form of bereavement as you say goodbye to the years of active fatherhood.

You know as you age that your daughter is far more likely to be looking after you than you are to be looking after her. You may have an increasing sense of your physical frailty, which reinforces the poignancy of your feeling. But if you are able to watch your son and daughter making their own way in the world, responding positively to setbacks and able to rely on and develop their own inner resources, then you can reflect on a job well done as a father. You have time now that you didn't have when they were younger to develop yourself. Moving on can be difficult because we often naturally resist change, but through change you may find the excitement of a new beginning.

a new generation

Your daughter gives birth to a beautiful daughter of her own, and you become a grandfather. You are plunged back into family life, but from a different perspective. How quickly the family has come around full circle and a new generation has begun. If you are feeling saddened by the onset of old age, you may taste the joy of new life in this child as particularly sweet. Many grandparents say that with their grandchildren they are able to experience the joys of being with young children without the responsibility of providing for them.

Tears such as loving fathers shed
Warm from my ageing eyes descend,
For joy, to think, that when I'm dead,
My son shall have mankind his friend.

GEORGE FREDREICH HANDEL (1685–1759)

picture credits

All commissioned photography by Debi Treloar

(unless stated otherwise)

Page 61 photography by Caroline Arber

Page 32, 52–53, 59 photography by Dan Duchars

Page 31 photography by Chris Tubbs

acknowledgments

I'd like to thank Alison East for three labors—and her love, support, and friendship.

The publishers would like to thank all those who kindly lent photographs from their family albums.

Every effort has been made to contact copyright holders; in the event of an inadvertent omission or error, please notify the editorial department at Ryland Peters & Small, Kirkman House, 12–14 Whitfield Street, London W1T 2RP, UK.